To:
_____

From:
_____

Date:
_____

Message:

_____
_____
_____
_____
_____

FOUNTAIN OF LIFE

Book of Christian Poems

&

Words of Wisdom

Marie-Pearl Addo

Fountain of Life
Copyright © Marie-Pearl Addo, 2014
by CreateSpace Self Publishing
www.createspace.com

Printed and bound by createspace.com

First published in Great Britain in 2009

ISBN 978-0-9556458-1-5

All rights reserved. No part of this publication may be reproduced in any form without prior permission of the author
mariepearl@hotmail.com

All Scriptures are quoted from the New International Version of the Bible

Dedication

Fountain of Life, Book of Christian Poems and Words of Wisdom is firstly dedicated to my Lord and Saviour Jesus Christ and the Holy Spirit for equipping me to write this book of poems.

Secondly, to my dear husband Robert Kingsley Afful who has been my silent supporter and has unknowingly triggered most of these poems. Thank you, Robert. I love you dearly. The poem – **Knowing You** is in honour of you.

Lastly, but by no means least I dedicate this book to my darling daughter Ayodele Joy Afful, and my friends Yvonne Naa Lamley Mills and Cynthia Naana Graham who have been my private audience at home. Thank you, girls for all your support and encouragement to publish another book of poems.

Proverbs 36:9
*For with you is the **fountain of life**, in your light we see light.*

Proverbs 13:14
*The teaching of the wise is a **fountain of life**, turning a man from the snares of destruction.*

TABLE OF CONTENTS

A MOTHER'S LOVE	8
A QUESTION OF FAITH	9
THE BATTLE IS WON	10-11
KNOWING YOU	12
CHANGING HANDS	13
THE STRUGGLE IS OVER	14
SOMETHING MIRACULOUS	15
THE UNTOUCHABLE	16
GLORY HAS DESCENDED	17
WATCHING OVER YOU	18
ENTER MY REST	19
FREEDOM ARRIVES	20
PARDONED	21
I STAND ACCUSED	22
LOOKING FORWARD	23
AFLAME	24
ENOUGH IS ENOUGH	25
NEVER TOO LATE	26
BLESS ME LORD	27
BLESS ME SOME MORE	28
I NEED YOUR BLESSING	29
THE MASTER'S PLAN	30
THE VESSEL	31
LEAVE IT ALL	32
COUNTERATTACK	33
WHO	34
BE STILL	35
LOOKING AHEAD	36
MEMORIES	37
THE STORM IS OVER NOW	38-39
IT IS NOT OVER	40
DECISIONS, DECISIONS, DECISIONS	41
BEAUTY FROM ABOVE	42
MY LIFE	43
TAKE A STAND	44

REIGN IN IT	45
MY REFUGE	46
PATH OF LIFE	47
MY LIGHT	48
BEAR IT ALL	49

A MOTHER'S LOVE

It's wonderful it's beautiful
And oh so divine to watch
a Mother look at her child
with such love in her eyes.

The look so tender and oh so sweet
will send tiny shivers right down
your spine, your mind and all.

A look that sends a thousand messages
all at once without a doubt; can warm
any heart whether soft or cold.

And if a Mother can show such
selfless love to a child, how much
more our Father in Heaven who teaches
us to love one another regardless
of how we feel.

A QUESTION OF FAITH

In life everything is possible for the
one who believes.

Don't wait dear friend to see before
you believe.

The journey of life is not by sight
but indeed by faith.

The wrong you see today can turn
around only if you hope and pray for
a turnaround.

Why don't you just call things that are not
as though they were and see things change
for the best in life.

THE BATTLE IS WON

The battle is won, the battle is won,
I hear a still voice say the battle is won.

The battle that has been waging
year on and on and as far as
I can recall.

The storms were raging, the waves
rose high as the sky. I had no where
to hide from the attacks of life.

I looked for peace but it was
light years away, something I say
of the good days of old, but not one
of today.

How did this raging storm
calm down so fast? How come
the waves are no where to be found.

The Lord heard my cry and
stretched forth his hands to calm
what seemed like an impossible
battle to fight.

Indeed, it's true what He tells us
in His Word – *'the battle is not yours but Mine'*
indeed.

Move on to the winning side
my friend, for it is not by your
own might or power at all, but
by His ability and will for your life.

KNOWING YOU

Loving you has brought out
a lot of mixed feelings in me
The strength I never imagined
I had, jumped out in me
Selfless thoughts and gesture are
now a part of me.

The years have taken its toll on us
but knowing the friend I have found
in you has caused me to stay on,
no matter the case.

I've learnt a thing or two from you,
you know. Although I may not have
uttered as much to you; if nothing at all,
your stance on integrity speaks for itself.

I may not be the perfect mate
for you, but I strive to make the
best of what we have together today.
I will be there when it's upwards
and forward all the way. I will be there
when the going gets tough and rough.

I just want you to know, you are treasured
through and through no matter what the
future holds for us. Remember that with God
we can only succeed in all we hope for.

CHANGING HANDS

The season we've heard so much
about is drawing nearer and nearer
each passing day.

We've heard it preached from times
of old that a time is coming when the
wealth of the wicked will be handed
over to the children of faith.

For years the wicked are said to
be gathering wealth for the righteous
ones and at God's own set time, the
transfer will take place, all for real.

It really is a wonder how this can be true
but indeed the Good Lord uses the foolish
things of this world to confound the wise.

The set time is nearer than you think
my friend, so get prepared if you are of
course on the winning side.

THE STRUGGLE IS OVER

I hear the words *'the struggle is over'*.
It sounds over and over in my ears.
'The struggle is over'.

The years of battle, of strain and strive
is no more indeed.

The labour of pain and lack is now a story
of the past.

A new beginning is on the horizon
of faith and no one can tell me otherwise I say.

My days of sweat, contention and toil
is forever gone.

With my head lifted high, I cry out and say
'My harvest is here, my harvest is here'.

The struggle, the struggle, I say the struggle
is over indeed!

SOMETHING MIRACULOUS

All the odds seem to be against me
these days; whatsoever I do
Every effort simply has become
a difficult task.

Nothing gives way no matter how much I try.
I push and push and to no avail at all.

I have seen these signs from the past,
if I can recall right; that in effect something
good is about to happen.

No matter how bad it looks today, I will keep
holding on to my faith, knowing that
with every passing hour my miracle is
about to happen for all to see.

THE UNTOUCHABLE

I may be walking about as everyone else,
but there is one thing you may not be
aware of ... I am untouchable!

It is said in the Word that *'no weapon that is formed against me shall ever prosper'*.

I am untouchable!

Yes, the attacks will come and go, but
I will tell you one thing for sure….
None of these weapons will ever prevail or
prosper against me..

I am untouchable!

There will surely be times of oppression
and depression when I may look down
and out, but when I fall, I shall arise
and the Lord has promised to be
my light in my times of darkness.

I am untouchable!

Nothing can touch me and bring me down
forever, for *greater is He that is in me than he that is in this world.*

I can confidently say I am untouchable!

GLORY HAS DESCENDED

I see glory all around me today
It seems the Heavens have opened
and poured down a blessing of grace.

My days of sorrow have vanished in a flash
and joy explodes like an erupted volcano
on fire.

Who ever thought this season would
pass away? The tension, the stress,
the strain and much more. All joining
forces to chase my dreams away.

The glory has descended ....
Oh yes! Indeed it has, to light up my
days of darkness and gloomy hours on end.

I hear a voice whisper in my ears
"Arise my daughter, arise and shine
for my glory of grace is upon you today
and has also come to stay.

WATCHING OVER YOU

I hold a staff and rod in hand and watch
every step you take along the way.

Once or twice you've strayed far from my fold
but grace has brought you back home time
and time again.

Learn to listen attentively to my voice my son
and heed to my call as I take a roll call of my
chosen ones on earth.

There may be wolves in your midst,
some in sheep's clothing and some without
but fear not, as I have promised never to
leave you no matter what.

I will watch over you, my son, even as you
slumber and sleep. No harm will come to you
if you learn to listen and heed to my voice.

ENTER MY REST

I just can't work it out today,
for some reason I seem to care less
come what may.

What made me shiver with fear yesterday
can't seem to ruffle my feathers no matter
how much it tries.

I radiate with joy when I really should despair
and cry, but try as I may I simply can't wipe
the smile with a tear.

What seemed like heavy weights on my
shoulders a short while ago now feels
as light as air.

Don't get me wrong, nothing has changed
but I just don't feel the weight for I have
passed it all on to the Lord who has promised
to bear my burdens daily.

Indeed, indeed I have entered the rest of God
and I'm enjoying the day that He has made.

FREEDOM ARRIVES

Who has held my children captive?
Free them and let them go!

Their time of bondage and slavery is over.
Today I break the shackles and chains and set them free.

Whom I set free, is free indeed. I know it comes as a dream and mystery to all.

But the set time is now and no matter how you try to hold them back; my chosen ones are at liberty today, I say.

PARDONED

In spite of it all ………..
He lifted me up and pardoned my sins.

He made me into a new creation for the world to see.

In spite of it all …………
He chose to bear all my pain, my sickness and all my disease.

He taught me to change my mindset and led me to victory.

In spite of it all ………….
He died in my place and saved me from destruction and going to hell.

He has prepared a place for me in Heaven when He calls me to glory.

I STAND ACCUSED

My fellow brethren point a finger at me
today and I stand accused.

Regardless of all that I am going through,
it's easily overlooked and I stand accused.

In spite of my pain, my turmoil, my secret
fears and dismay; I stand accused.

The friend that I thought I had, has
a stone in hand ready to throw at me
for it is believed that no matter my plea;
I stand accused.

In life it's easy to lay down rules for another
but to justify yourself when it comes to
your turn.

I look not to man to gain my pardon,
instead I look up to Christ who took my place
and declared me not guilty no matter what you
say or think today.

I am saved by faith through God's grace and
mercy and that settles the case for me.
I no longer stand accused. I utter *'Not Guilty'*
as my rightful plea.

LOOKING FORWARD

Look forward always and don't look back,
for what has already happened can never be
changed no matter how much you try.

All you can do is learn lessons from the past
and history of your life, and by the grace
of God hope that all lost years will be restored
and old things made new.

There certainly is no need to think what could have been,
for the Good Lord has a unique plan for you
that match no other plan on earth.

Look forward my friend, not
side to side or backwards still,
for the future looks bright
when you are on the winning
side with Christ.

AFLAME

I feel the heat of burning
coals on me no matter where
I turn these days.

The hands of the Refiner
seems very heavy on me and
I have nowhere to hide
anyway I say.

I know if I am able to withstand this period to
the end,
I will come out as pure as
gold in the midst of hay.

I will hold on and stay in the
heat of the moment and be
the worthy vessel my Master
can use today.

ENOUGH IS ENOUGH

It's been a season of afflictions and trails,
temptations, oppression and all.

I think to myself and shout out loud
'enough is enough'.

Some of these arrows came when my back
was turned and unaware. I was a target on
show on a battlefield.

Although, I had a choice to react right on,
I chose to look up and respond with a
tested word in season.

Try as you may, I am anchored
on a rock and standing on a solid
foundation for life.

Enough is enough.

I wield the sword of the Spirit to combat
your attacks and remember; it is written
that *'no weapon formed against me shall prosper'*
and that's for sure.

NEVER TOO LATE

It's never too late when the Good Judge
is around and working on your case
behind the scenes.

Sometimes it may seem that the odds
are against you and all hell is breaking loose
here and there. But believe me when I say
'it's never too late' for the Master Planner
to act on your behalf.

The clock is ticking and you seem to be
running out of time, but remember that
He is the Creator of all as well as time
and He holds it all in His mighty hands.

Do not be afraid. Do not fear or be dismayed,
for with Him all things are possible and he is
well able to turn the seemingly impossible
to an absolute possible right on time just
for you.

BLESS ME LORD

Lord bless me with the faithfulness
and righteousness of Abraham and enable
me to believe and hold onto your word.

Lord bless me with the caring and kind nature
of Boaz who showed great compassion to
Ruth when she faced lack in her life.

I want the courage that Caleb had to enter
the promised land and his devotion to you,
Lord.

Lord bless me with the close fellowship that
David had with you coupled with his bravery
and trust in you to bring him to victory come
what may.

Lord bless me with the divine favour Esther
had before you and men in the midst of
great trouble.

I am looking for the humility that Gideon had
that caused him to be empowered to become
a man of valour and a warrior great in battle.

Lord bless me and help me to be a blessing to
others!

BLESS ME SOME MORE

Oh Lord bless me with the sincerity and
persistence of Hannah as she believed
and awaited her request to be granted.

Lord bless me with words of knowledge
and oracles as you blessed Isaiah; who foretold
the salvation of God in his days of old.

I want you to be with me at all times as you
were with Joseph and give me success in all
that I do, having favour every step of the way.

Lord bless me as you blessed Lazarus and
raised him back to life. Let your healing and
resurrection power flow through me I pray.

Lord, bring out the leader in me as you
did in Moses; who led your children from
the land of slavery to your promised land;
a land full of milk and honey.

I seek your blessings day by day. Lord, make
me into whom you created me to be.

I NEED YOUR BLESSING

Lord, I want you to bless me with the boldness that the prophet Nathan had to confront evil and speak your word just as it is, with no fear at all.

Lord bless me with the willingness of Obed-Edom who was specially chosen to take care of the ark of the Lord.

I want a repentant heart like Paul, with boldness and confidence in the things and ways of God.

Lord bless me as you blessed Ruth, with humility and loyalty as she clung onto Naomi and followed her instructions in life.

Oh, Lord bless me with your wisdom and wealth as you blessed Solomon; the king who ruled with such wisdom and counsel it caused people to travel from far and wide.

Lord, I desire a teachable spirit as Timothy had. Bless all my descendants and I as you did for Lois and Eunice right down the line.

THE MASTER'S PLAN

We go through life with our own agenda
and plan for the days that lay ahead;
not realising that God holds our life in
His hands.

No matter how good a plan we think we have
we should remember what the Word rightfully
says *"…many are the plans of man but it is the
Lord's that will prevail"*.

Isn't it best to live according to His plan
than follow our own choices in life, playing
guessing games along the way and taking part
in trial and error all the way.

People say *'experience is the best teacher'* in life but
should we really go through uncalled for
experiences when we could easily talk to our
Father in Heaven; who holds the master plan
for our lives.

I'd say let's put all our plans aside and ask what
His purposes and plans are for our lives.

THE VESSEL

The vessel looked old and cracked and not
fit for the Master's use. The wear and tear
of years gone by, told the world a tale of
abuse, misuse and battering and all.

It was often overlooked on the shelf on
which it stood and rejection seemed like
the norm of the day.

Not a soul knew, but the Master had a plan for
the one that looked forsaken and outdated
to say the least.

Suddenly, this vessel was placed in the Potter's
hand and broken and moulded into a beautiful
vessel of worth. He poured in His treasure
and made it anew, perfect and equipped for
the Master's use.

LEAVE IT ALL

Leave it all in the hands of God when you've tried your best and nothing seems to come out of it. He always makes a way where there seems to be no way.

Leave it all in the hands of Jehovah when the door shuts in your face and you know not here to turn. He knows the end from the beginning.

Leave it all, I say leave it all, when all you do is good but you get evil in return. The Good Lord knows and will reward you in time.

Leave it all in the hands of our Lord when your dreams and desires seem shattered and grey. He is able to turn the unseen to seen. Just watch the space.

COUNTERATTACK

It seems the odds are against
me wherever I turn these days. Don't ask
me why?

The storm is rushing towards me, the waves
are raging higher and high. I seem to hear
an invisible sound of roaring from a distance
afar, although I see no predator about.

The arrows are evidently aimed at me.
The cunning plot of an adversary lurks in the
shadows of my life.

But in the midst of all this chaos of war,
all I feel is a peace that beats all human
understanding.

I am not moved by what I feel, hear or see,
for I know whom I have believed, in all of this.
It is true that in life, attacks will come and go
but my assurance is, come what may, there is
none that can hurt me forevermore.

WHO?

Who placed this wall before me today;
and thought it could surely block my chance
of moving ahead?

With the help of the Lord I will leap over in time.

Who says limitations can put me down and
out?

With God there is always another plan to cause me to succeed.

Who put this barricade in my way and thought
there was no way. I can jump this hurdle and
survive.

*With God I know He makes a way where there seems
to be no way at all.*

In life there will always be obstructions in
the way, but with faith and trust in our Father
in Heaven you can only succeed and prosper
in life.

BE STILL

Be still, be still I hear a soothing voice say
'Be still and know that I am God'.

There is nothing that is impossible for me
to do or too hard for me at all.

When the trials and troubles in life, hit home,
you need hope to move on day by day.

What can this world offer you, to give you
the peace and security that you crave?

Money, possessions, status and all, can't give
you the peace and the fulfilment that you
so desire.

Jesus is the answer no matter what you think.
Turn it all to Him and get what I mean.

LOOKING AHEAD

There is too much goodness ahead to
look back on past failures and woes, I say.

I have set my eyes on what lays ahead
and purposely forgotten what is behind
and past.

No matter how much I try, I can't change
history as it so stands.

But yes, I can hope for the best in my present
state and now; and take bold steps of faith
as the Lord leads me on.

Whatever the future has in store for me,
I know by God's grace, I can face tomorrow
any day.

MEMORIES

As I walked down memory lane today,
the thoughts of yesterday's saga lingered
on and on.

The countless joy experienced in years
gone by, all mingled with spells of pain,
of hurt and forget-me-not days.

It's simply amazing how I overcame those days
of grief. All I now know is that the power
to do so lies not in me but Christ in me.

THE STORM IS OVER NOW

The chaos of yesterday seems to be settling down fast.

What seemed like a turbulent storm and a fiery furnace all packed into one has died down and stillness has taken its turn.

How I managed to go through the storm; I know not how.

All I know is that every step of the way; the Master was with me and when the time was right He stretched out His hands and stilled the storm.

My Master spoke, but a word and calmed the waves.

He whispered softly in my ears "my daughter, my daughter the tide has come home to settle."

Indeed, His word is so true when He says;
He will be with me when I go through deep waters and great trouble.

What more can I ask for when the Lord has assured me of protection even in the fire of oppression.

All I can say is – come what may the Lord
is my refuge in my times of woe.

IT IS NOT OVER

Don't write me off yet
Don't give up on me
Don't pass me by
For it is not over yet.

It may seem that I am running
out of time.

It may seem nothing good will come
out of me no matter how much I try.

It may seem that the race is finished
and I haven't even begun.

But wait a moment for me; for my time
is coming soon and my season is drawing
nigh I say.

Watch the space for great manifestation of
a bright new beginning.

It is not over yet until God says it is!

DECISIONS, DECISIONS, DECISIONS

The decisions we make in life paves the way for our tomorrow.

The choices we make gives birth to our destiny, be it good or bad.

The Lord has given us all a free will in life for the days that lay ahead.

He places it all before us. Life and death choose what you may.

In life its pointless thinking, you can live your life anyhow and settle on all that fate throws at you.

Let's follow the plans the Lord has for us, for He has promised it is good and not evil for an expected end and a future too.

BEAUTY FROM ABOVE

As I walk the sandy shores by day,
I can't help but marvel at all that the
Good Lord has created.

The tiny, delicate sand that stretches
from shore to shore looks just so perfect
and fine.

The pebbles; they come in all sizes and shapes
both rough and smooth.

The waves that can roar and rage high up
and sometimes lie still and calm awaiting
orders from on high.

The creatures both great and small;
all share and dwell in the vast waters
spreading far and wide.

Oh what a wonder, a picture of sheer divine
perfection. Lord, I stand in awe of your
creation and works for all mankind to
use and enjoy.

MY LIFE

Every breathe I take is a prayer to say
thank you for giving me life today.

Every step I take I know you've ordered
for your divine purpose and plan.

Every move I make is just by your grace
and mercy that follows me day by day.

Every word I speak, I pray it comes to
build and edify those who talk and listen
to me.

I lift my whole life and being into your hands
and ask that you bless me dear Lord as I plod
on in life.

TAKE A STAND

Amidst all the turmoil and strife in this world, learn to take a stand no matter what life throws at you.

Although you wrestle not against flesh and blood, stand on the word of God and stumble not.

No matter the pressures and trials in life, remember that with God all things are possible and take a firm stand not to doubt.

Look not around and take no heed of what you hear. Take a stand and focus on God - who holds your life in His hands.

REIGN IN IT

Even in the midst of all this chaos
I can see the light of God shinning tenderly
on me.

Leading me and guiding me along the paths
on which to walk.

I hear the voice of God propelling me
right on to success and bringing me
comfort where comfort is not.

I feel the peace of God deep inside of me
and can't help but live it out right in the
midst of it all.

No matter what plans this chaos had in mind,
I've had no unrest but a sound mind through
it all.

For with God on my side nothing and no one
can be against me and this is for sure.

MY REFUGE

Shield me Oh Jehovah God.
Shield me from the pressures of life.

Remove the heavy burden I face and still
the fears that arise to push me down.

I look all around and search and search
but find no answers to questions at hand.

I know my answers come not from worldly
pleasures but can only be found in your
presence and love.

PATH OF LIFE

The Lord has shed His light on me
to expel what seems like darkness
all around.

The steps I take each day I breathe
are now those of one who knows the way.

My days of stumbling and trials are over;
for the Lord is guiding and protecting
me along my path.

Indeed, I'll fear not as the lights go out,
for my source is one that quenches not.

MY LIGHT

As I arise and shine today,
I take heed of what the Lord
has said.

Indeed, I feel and see His glory
upon my life.

And no matter how it looks
or feels today, I know I am
a victor and not a victim in life.

My day may look dark to you; with no
way out of this turmoil and mess.

But I see the light, the Lords sheds on
my path and His guiding hands that
lead me on the way to go.

BEAR IT ALL

At times it seems the burden is
way too heavy to bear.

But when I remember what the
Lord went through for my sake,
I realise my load is not as heavy
 as I think.

The betrayal from one, so close,
the persecution in the face of good
deeds; the slander, the pain, the hurt
feelings and all.

The unfaithfulness of those He trusted
and loved so dear.

The dishonour, disrespect and feelings
of despair; My Saviour went through
all and uttered no complaint at all.

By His grace I carry this burden so light
as compared to what my Saviour bore
for me.

He's been there and done that and
that's for sure.

www.ingramcontent.com/pod-product-compliance
Lightning Source LLC
Chambersburg PA
CBHW061302040426
42444CB00010B/2482